Instant Pot CookBook For Vegetarian Legends ®

Pressure Cooker Guide

Amy Wilson

Table of Contents

Introduction

I would like to take a few moments to thank and commend you for downloading your personal copy of the *Instant Pot Cookbook For Vegetarian Legends ®: Pressure Cooker Guide.*

Time moves quickly and with that time comes technology which has introduced many gadgets for kitchens dating all the way back to 1952 when your ancestors were amazed by the West Bend invention of the Electric Bean Pot. In 1936 Irving Naxon, an inventor attempted to patent a cooker inspired by his Grandmother but failed to receive the required patent. In 1940 he received the patent for the Naxon Beanery 'low and slow' cooker.

The new invention of the Instant Pot came in 2010 provided by one of the founders, Robert Wang, who really opened the door. Since that time, three new models have been improved and released.

The Instant Pot will combine qualities which include a yogurt maker, slow cooker, rice cooker, electric pressure cooker, sauté pan, steamer, and so many more features the competition cannot match.

The recipes will begin to intrigue you the *instant* you open the first chapter. You will want to stop what you are doing, visit the supermarket, and purchase each of the ingredients you will need to tempt and satisfy each of your taste buds! On the other hand; if you are already a vegetarian, you can just begin your new adventures.

You will be provided with many recipes from breakfast to dinner as well as a few fairly healthy desserts. Most of them will provide you with healthy choices, and some will just be so yummy, you will forget about the calorie counts for just a few minutes.

The professionals have taken out all of the guesswork with the proven steps and guidelines on how to enjoy your food while taking less time to prepare it.

I sincerely hope you enjoy each chapter as you learn the many ways you can choose to eat healthier on a vegetarian diet plan. I hope you enjoy each and every meal!

Chapter 1: The Vegetarian Plan

This section is dedicated to relevant information which will be useful during your vegetarian experience.

Elements of the Vegetarian Diet

Vegetarian diets encompass more than just vegetables and fruits. Vegetarian diets consist of three foremost classifications based on the types of food consumed.

- **Lacto-Vegetarian:** This individual does not include poultry, fish, meat or eggs. Broccoli and dark green leafy vegetables are an excellent choice for calcium. Nonetheless, they will eat dairy products, including items such as yogurt, cheese, and milk. The diet will also contain fruits vegetables, herbs, nuts, grains, seeds, fungi, roots, and kefir
- **Lacto-Ovo**: This particular vegetarian diet only excludes fish, meat, and poultry, whereas on this plan the dairy products and eggs are allowed. Greek yogurt and eggs are an excellent source of protein.
- ***Vegan:*** On the flip side of the menu; a vegan does not eat, fish, poultry, meat, dairy products or eggs.

Necessary for the Vegetarian Diet Plan

Essential Grains

Five to seven servings of grain daily and should rule with at least one-half of the daily serving which includes pasta, bread, wheat, rice, barley, and oats.

Additional nutrients can be derived from the grain food groups such as zinc, iron, and vitamin B12, which a vegetarian may be lacking because the bulk of the nutrients are generally acquired from seafood and meat sources.

Proteins

Five daily servings should be delegated to protein-rich foods including soy, nuts, beans, and legumes.

Iron deficiencies are also common and can be provided by peas, dry beans, fortified oatmeal, lentils, spinach, tofu, and soybeans.

Vitamin C helps absorb iron which comes in foods such as oranges, strawberries, tomatoes, and broccoli.

Vegetables and Fruits

At least six to eight servings of veggies are on the agenda as well as three to four fruits daily.

Fats

To ensure proper brain development, your body requires a small amount of dietary fat. Two servings should be included that are high in the omega-3 fatty acids. One serving includes two tablespoons of nut butter, a one-ounce portion of seeds or nuts, or one teaspoon of canola or olive oil.

The Story Behind Beans

These are just several reasons you need to include beans in your diet besides being low-fat and having no cholesterol.

Beans are high in:

- Vitamins
- Carbohydrates

- Protein
- Minerals
- Insoluble and Soluble Fiber

They have also been reported by the USDA as reducing many chronic diseases including cancer, heart disease, obesity, and diabetes.

Health Benefits of the Vegetarian Diet

If you realize the similarity in what beans do for you; just add more veggies to your list for these additional benefits; reduced risk of diabetes, heart disease, dementia, and improved moods to name just a few. More will be explained further later.

Lacto-Vegetarian Diet Plans

These are just several examples of how you can still maintain a healthy and fulfilling meal as a lacto-vegetarian. These are two days of what your meals should be like:

Day One: Breakfast, Lunch, Dinner, and Snacks:

Orange juice
1 slice whole grain toast with one teaspoon butter
2 boiled or scrambled eggs
Large salad with orange dressing

- Feta Cheese
- Seeds and Raisins
- Whole grain roll
- Some berries with plain yogurt

Cashew and Vegetable Stir-fry

Homemade low-fat muffin

Handful of almonds (small amount)

Lacto-Vegetarian Guidelines Day One:

It is best to use butter instead of margarine as long as you use it sparingly since it contains coloring, modified fats, chemically altered elements, and preservatives. Butter only has salt and cream. Your intestinal health is supported with plain yogurt with its 'friendly bacterial cultures.' Fresh fruit is preferred because the sugar will cancel out the benefits of yogurt.

Add some brown rice to any meal with some fresh-squeezed fruit and vegetable drinks. With all of the juicers on the market today; it is such a healthy choice, and easy. Not only will it taste fabulous, but it is also packed with enzymes, minerals, and vitamins. Follow up with a minimum of six to eight glasses of 'plain' clear water.

Day Two: Breakfast, Lunch, Dinner, and Snacks

Homemade cinnamon and raisins oatmeal is a great start.

A glass of rice, almond, or cow's milk is excellent along with some fruit juice of your choice.

A Turkey and Veggie sandwich with some light mayonnaise is great to build a sandwich made from a slice or red onion, tomatoes, and some sprouts. Put it on 2 slices of multigrain bread with a slice of dill pickle on the side of the dish.

Have a handful of grapes with a glass of V-8 juice.

For dinner; enjoy some tacos which are nutritious and save tons of time in preparation.

Snacks can include some homemade trail mix along with some plain yogurt, a sliced banana, and a sprinkle of cinnamon.

Lacto-Vegetarian Guidelines: Day Two

Steer away from the instant oatmeal and opt for the stovetop method. Many of the nutrients can be lost when they are more refined for instant packaging. Use a 'real' mayonnaise versus 'Miracle Whip' types since they have preservatives and sugar added.

Don't skip your snack time. You can keep the metabolism pumping when you maintain the food at an even rate.

Consider Iron Content and the Vegetarian Lifestyle

Many people believe vegetarian diets lack iron, but this is not true. Studies have proven vegetarians who consume a balanced diet, do not have any more issues with iron-deficiency anemia than their fellow contenders the 'meat' eaters.

These are some of the (milligram) sources your plan offers you for iron:

Iron-fortified cereals (1 ounces): 4-8

Blackstrap molasses (one tablespoon): 3.5

Chickpeas (1/2 cup, canned): 2

Dried fruits: apricots, peaches (3 ounces): 2

Tomato paste (2 ounces): 2

Prune juice (8 ounces): 3

Beans: kidney, black (1/2 cup): 2

Figs (5): 2

For most adult women, approximately 15 milligrams each day should be included from iron. Post-menopausal women and men should consume around 10 milligrams daily. For lactating, pregnant women, and children will require more. It is best to get your physician's advice to ensure it matches your health requirements.

Chapter 2: Vegetarian Breakfasts

Steamed Korean Style Eggs

Ingredients

1 large egg
Chopped scallions
1/3 cup cold water
Pinch each of:
- Ground Pepper
- Salt
- Garlic powder
- Sesame seeds

Instructions

Beat the eggs and add the water; whisk together in a small container.

Strain the combination into a heat-proof dish using a fine mesh strainer. Combine the remainder of ingredients, blending well, and set it to the side.

Empty a cup of water into the IP.

Place the steamer basket into the Instant Pot. Put the mixture into the basket.

Tightly close the lid and shut the vent valve. Use the manual setting on high for five minutes. Allow the QR when the timer buzzes.

Serve right away with a dish of hot rice.

Yields: The recipe is for one person, but you can add as many as needed.

Hard Boiled Eggs

This is the simplest way to have some boiled eggs when you are in a hurry. Only prepare as many as you need. It doesn't matter how many eggs you cook; the process is the same. Just be sure none of them are cracked.

Instructions

1. Place the basket inside the pot and pour one cup of water into the Instant Pot.
2. Put the eggs on the basket and tightly close the lid/vent valve.
3. Use the high pressure, manual setting:
    a. Runny Yolk: Poached egg: One minute
    b. Soft Boiled: Four minutes
    c. Hard Boiled: Five minutes
4. Remove and put the eggs in cold water and refrigerate when cooled.

Note: For hard to peel eggs, use one cup for poaching and remove the struggle. You can reheat eggs on the steam function for one-minute to have them as if they had just been poached.

IP Oatmeal

The only ingredients needed for this particular treat are three cups of water and one cup of steel cut oats. How simple is that?

Optional Toppings: Cinnamon and Apples

Instructions

1. Put the oats and water into the Instant Pot. Close the lid and vent.

2. Use the manual buttons and arrows—to cook the oats for three minutes.
3. You can unplug the pot and allow the pressure to release naturally.
4. Open the top and stir the oats.
5. Garnish with the toppings of your choice and enjoy a delicious and nutritious breakfast.

Yields: Two to Three Servings

Vegan Yogurt

Ingredients

1 Quart Soy milk
1 Package Vegan Yogurt culture

Instructions

1. Combine the milk and the culture and mix well. Pour the mixture into a one-quart size wide-mouth Mason jar. You can also *not* use a lid or use other containers as long as they are heat-proofed.
2. Select the yogurt function on the IP using the (-) and (+) function for 12 hours.
3. For the pressure valve; it can be open or sealed for this one.
4. Once the time is complete; take the jar/jars from the Instant Pot and securely place the lids on each one.
5. Let them cool and refrigerate a minimum of six hours.

Wheat and Veggie Breakfast

Ingredients

2 cups white wheat berries (soaked overnight)
6 ½ cups water (use the soak water)
2-3 tablespoons butter/oil
1 tablespoon salt

2 cups sliced carrots

2 medium potatoes (sliced/cubed)

2-4 garlic cloves (smashed) optional

5 stalks of celery

1/8 teaspoon thyme

1 tsp. poultry seasoning or another favorite seasoning

Instructions

1. In a pan, sauté the carrots and potatoes using 2 to 3 tablespoons of butter/oil. Saute until browned.
2. Program the Instant Pot using the 'multi-grain' setting to cook the potatoes, wheat, and carrots.
3. Add the sautéed veggies and spices.
4. You can cook on the warm setting for about 30 minutes to let the flavors mingle or eat now.
5. Garnish with some flat-leaf parsley or serve with plain yogurt.

Note: Soak two cups of white wheat berries overnight with plenty of water.

You can have this for any meal and is also delicious after it is cool and has been refrigerated. You can also add more garlic if desired.

Chapter 3: Vegetarian Lunches

Penne Pasta

Ingredients

2 ¼ cups Penne pasta
1 small sliced onion
Optional: 1 small diced shallot
3 minced garlic cloves
12 sliced white mushrooms
1 thickly sliced zucchini squash
1 Pinch of each:
- Dried basil
- Dried oregano

Dash of Sherry wine
Kosher salt & Black Pepper

Olive oil

Ingredients: Pasta Sauce:

1 C. unsalted vegetable stock (+) 2 C. water
1 (4 ½ ounce) can tomato paste
2 tablespoons light soy sauce

Instructions

1. Make sure you preheat the Instant Pot before it is time to prepare your meal. It should register as 'HOT' before you add any ingredients.
2. *Note*: Saute the squash with 1 Tbsp. of olive oil and set to the side. Pour one tablespoon of oil into the pot, making

sure to cover the entire surface of the bottom. Toss in the onion and shallot with a pinch of pepper and salt.

3. Continue occasionally stirring until browned, and toss in the garlic for about thirty seconds. Combine the oregano basil, mushrooms, and squash to the pot and cook one more minute.
4. Pour the wine into the pot and deglaze to get all of the tasty brown bits from the bottom using a wooden spoon. Pour in one cup of the stock, water, and soy sauce.
5. Empty the Penne into the sauce adding the tomato paste on top of the pasta and combine. Be sure everything is under the sauce.
6. Set the IP to high-pressure for four minutes.
7. Turn off for five minutes before you do a quick release.
8. Taste the pasta. If it seems too hard, simply close the top and let the juices absorb the hardness until you have reached the right amount of doneness. Add the crunch squash if you prepared it for the dish.

Yields: Serves Two to Four

Lentil Plant-Based Pasta

Ingredients

3 garlic cloves (peeled, whole or smashed)
1 chopped small yellow onion
1 cup veggie broth
½ cup raw cashews (Presoak if a high-power blender isn't used)
1 teaspoon light miso paste
2 Tablespoons nutritional yeast flakes

Lentils

½ cup fresh lentils (sorted and rinsed)
1 cup vegetable broth/water
1 small bay leaf
2 teaspoons dried thyme

1 (28-ounce) can tomatoes (whole - diced & crushed fire roasted)

Pasta

1 Pound ditalini pasta or another favorite

Instructions

1. Pulse the tomatoes if they are whole using a high-powered blender.
2. Use the sauté function on the Instant Pot to sauté the onions until slightly browned. Pour in the broth or water, stirring as you add the garlic. Saute for one or two more minutes.
3. Use the blender (high-powered)—add the garlic, sautéed onions, one cup vegetable broth, cashews, miso paste, and nutritional yeast—blending until smooth. Set to the side.
4. *In the Instant Pot*: Add one cup veggie broth, bay leaf, thyme, and lentils. Set for six minutes using the high-pressure setting; quick release. (The lentils will be slightly undercooked.)
5. Add the remainder of water and sauté with the lentils, bring it to a boil.
6. Add the salt and crushed tomatoes, to a simmer. Combine the pasta and stir.
7. Set the manual, low-pressure setting for ten minutes and quick release.
8. Add the cashew cream to the pot, stir, and wait several minutes for the mixture to thicken.

Enjoy the tasty meal!

Lentil Bolognese

Ingredients

1 Cup Beluga black lentils
1 yellow onion (diced)
3 medium carrots (minced)

1 small can tomato paste

1 can (28-ounce) tomatoes (fire roasted & chopped)

4 minced garlic cloves

2 tablespoons dry Italian seasonings

4 cups water

Red pepper flakes (to taste)

Balsamic vinegar

Pepper and salt

Instructions

1. Use the liner of the Instant pot and add everything—Omit the balsamic vinegar, pepper, and salt. Blend everything well and close the lid and the steam release knob.
2. Set the Pot to manual for 15 minutes.
3. When the timer is completed, do a natural release (10 minutes).
4. Open the lid, give it a drizzle of the balsamic and stir.
5. Serve over your favorite type of pasta.

Lentil Tacos

Ingredients

4 cups water

2 cups dry brown lentils

4 ounces tomato sauce

½ teaspoon cumin

1 teaspoon each:

- Chili powder
- Onion powder
- Salt
- Garlic powder

Instructions

1. Place all of the ingredients into the IP and stir completely.

2. Close the lid and be sure you have it sealed.
3. Using the manual function button and arrows (+) and (-), set the timer on the pot for fifteen minutes. Turn the IP off and release the pressure.
4. Open the pot carefully and stir. Let it cool for a few minutes.

This is delicious as part of a burrito salad or a soft/crunchy taco.

Quinoa Salad Wrap

Ingredients

1 cup diced cucumber

1 to 2 cups cooked chickpeas

4 cups cooked quinoa

½ cup bell pepper (yellow or red)

¼ cup diced red onion

¼ teaspoon garlic powder

½ cup diced tomatoes

1 tablespoon red wine vinegar

¼ cup (approximately) Zest and Juice of one lemon

Directions

1. Thoroughly combine each of the ingredients using a large container
2. Chill before it's time to eat so the flavors have plenty of time to mingle

Serving Suggestions

Use this as a side dish, like a green salad for added protein, or part of a wrap. You can also have some stuffed with raw spinach, and add the salad to the tortilla.

Note: Quinoa contains all of the nutrients you would normally receive if you chose to eat meat.

Summertime Boiled Peanut Salad

Ingredients

1 Lb. Raw peanuts (shelled)
2 cups of water
1 bay leaf
¼ cup each:
- diced celery
- diced hot peppers

½ cup each:
- diced sweet onion
- diced green pepper

2 Tbsp. Olive oil
¼ t. ground black pepper
¾ t. salt

Instructions

Blanch the peanuts in boiling salted water for one minute, and drain. Remove the skins and throw them away.

Cook the peanuts with the two cups of water and the bay leaf. Manually set the Instant pot for twenty minutes, or until softened.

In a large mixing container, combine the diced veggies and peanuts.

Combine the pepper, salt, lemon juice, and oil. Pour it over the salad and toss to mix.

Soups

Butternut Squash & Curry Soup

Ingredients

2 garlic cloves

1 large chopped onion

1 T. curry powder

1 ½ tsp. sea salt (fine)

1 (3-Pound) Butternut squash

1 tsp. olive oil

½ C. coconut milk/coconut cream

3 C. water

Optional Garnishes:

- Dried cranberries
- Hulled pumpkin seeds

Instructions

1. Cut the squash into one-inch cubes, or use some you have already frozen. Mince the cloves.
2. Use the sauté function and warm the oil; toss in the onions and sauté approximately eight minutes. Blend in the curry powder and garlic for about a minute.
3. Turn off the Pot. Add the squash, water, and salt. Close the top making sure the seal is also closed.
4. Choose the 'soup' function and let it cook for thirty minutes on the high-pressure setting.
5. You can quick release or wait it out for the ten minutes or so.
6. Pour it from the pot and blend it until smooth with a food processor or blender.
7. Return it to the Pot and pour in the coconut milk/cream.
8. Top with some dried cranberries, a pinch of salt, and some hulled pumpkin seeds.

Note: The leftovers are good for about one week in the refrigerator.

Yields: Four to Six Servings

Indo-Chinese Corn Soup

Ingredients

1 C. minced each minced:

- carrot
- cabbage

2 ½ cups corn kernels
2 t. sesame oil
1 Tbsp. Soy sauce
5 cups vegetable broth
2 tsp. grated ginger
1 ½ teaspoons ground cumin
2 tsp. minced garlic

Optional Spice: Ground pepper

Directions

1. Mix all of the components on the list into the Instant Pot—except for the pepper.
2. Use the high-pressure setting for ten minutes. Natural release the pressure on the IP.
3. Use about three cups of the soup and blend to thicken; return it to the pot.
4. Add a pinch of pepper or other flavorings.

Yields: Four servings

Instant Pot Saag

This is an Indian version of creamed spinach dish that is full of many nutrients. It is even better the second day.

Ingredients

1 Lb. rinsed mustard leaves
1 Lb. rinsed spinach

2 medium carrots

2 medium diced onions

4 minced garlic cloves

2-inch knob minced ginger

2 Tbsp. Ghee

2 tsp. salt

1 tsp. each:

- cumin
- garam masala
- coriander

Pinch of dried fenugreek leaves (kasoori methi)

½ tsp. each:

- black pepper
- turmeric
- cayenne

Instructions

1. Program the Instant Pot with the sauté button to melt the ghee.
2. Blend the ginger, garlic, onion, and other spices to the Pot—stirring for about two to three minutes.
3. Toss in the spinach, and continue to stir. As soon as the spinach wilts; add the mustard greens.
4. Push in the 'keep warm-cancel' button; put the lid on, and press the 'poultry' function for fifteen minutes.
5. Once the Instant Pot pressure releases; add the mixture into a blender and mix to the desired consistency.
6. Return it to the pot and push the 'keep warm' function until you are ready to serve dinner.

Garnish with a spoonful of ghee.

Notes: More ghee will be needed for serving. You may also want to add a small amount of corn starch or potato starch to thicken the soup. Add a small amount of the saag in a bowl and cream the starch in by mixing until it is dissolved. Pour it back into the sagg and mix it in well. This should thicken the soup to what you like.

Split Pea Soup

Ingredients

1 medium diced sweet potato
5 cups water
½ cup navy beans
1 cup split peas
3 bay leaves
½ teaspoon liquid smoke
Pepper and Salt
¼ - ½ cup nutritional yeast

Instructions

1. Combine the sweet potato, water, split peas, bay leaves, navy beans, and liquid smoke in the Instant Pot.
2. Use the high-pressure function for twenty minutes. Do a natural release.
3. Toss in the pepper, salt, and nutritional yeast. Adjust the seasonings as desired.

Yields: Four to Six Servings

Veggie & Lentil Soup

Ingredients

6 small potatoes
1 cup onions (diced)
3 cups chopped broccoli
3 large sliced carrots
2 quarts water
1 cup dry lentils
1 tsp. each:

- Garlic powder
- Salt
- Onion powder

1 bay leaf

½ teaspoon each:

- Black pepper
- Thyme
- Paprika

Instructions

1. Toss all of the chopped vegetables into the Instant Pot.
2. Throw in the lentils after they have been sorted and rinsed.
3. Blend in the seasonings and pour the water into the pot.
4. Close the top, making sure you seal the vent.
5. Use the arrows (-) and (+) to set manually for 15minutes.
6. When the cycle is finished; you can unplug the unit and let the Instant Pot release the pressure naturally. After 10 minutes, you can release the remainder of the pressure in the pot.
7. Discard the bay leaf and serve.

3-Bean Chili

Ingredients

2/3 Cups each:

- Dried red beans
- Pinto beans
- Black beans

OR 1 ½ Cups each of the cooked beans (out of the can: drained)

Saute Ingredients

2 cups chopped onions

1 t. cumin seeds

1 Tbsp. Minced garlic

Add-In Ingredients

3 ½ cups boiling vegetable broth/water
1 (de-seeded and chopped) red bell pepper
¾ cup chopped carrots (2 sticks)
¼ cup celery (1 stick)
1 ½ teaspoon each

- Cumin
- Dried oregano

2 tablespoons mild chili powder
½ teaspoon coriander
1 teaspoon smoked paprika
Optional: ¼ teaspoon cayenne pepper

After Instant Pot Cooking Ingredients (14.5 oz.) 1 Can each:

- Diced tomatoes
- Tomato sauce

Garnish Suggestions:

- Cashew sour cream
- Fresh parsley
- Fresh cilantro
- Nutritional yeast
- Green onions
- Black olives
- Roast red peppers
- Choice of hot sauce
- Shredded vegan cheese (see Ch. 5 for the recipe)

Instructions

1. Rinse all of the beans, combine, and cover with water. Soaking overnight is best, but for a minimum of eight hours is recommended. Rinse and drain again after soaking.

2. Use the sauté function for five minutes on the Instant Pot; toss in the onion, cumin seeds, and minced garlic. Add the water/vegetable broth to avoid burning (as needed).
3. Blend in the remainder of the ingredients; saving the tomato sauce and diced tomatoes for after the cooking cycle. Mix well, lock and secure the lid, with the vent valve closed.
4. Use the high-pressure manual setting for 12 minutes (for six minutes if you used canned beans).
5. Once the 12/6 minutes are completed; allow a natural pressure release.
6. Blend in the can of tomato sauce and paste. Let the lid stay off of the Instant Pot as the chili cools.

Note: If you want thicker chili; blend one to two cups of the chili mixture in a high-speed blender/mixer. Add it back into the Instant Pot.

Garnishes:

Saute 2 cups of chopped onions, 1 teaspoon of cumin seeds with a tablespoon of minced garlic; yummy!

Yields: Six to Eight Servings

Chapter 4: Vegetarian Dinners

Asian Steamed Dumplings

Ingredients

1 Tbsp. Vegetable broth/small amount of water/vegetable broth
1 cup white/shiitake mushrooms
½ cup shredded carrot
1 ½ cups minced cabbage
2 Tbsp. soy sauce
1 t. fresh grated ginger
1 Tbsp. rice wine vinegar
Optional: 1 t. sesame oil
12 round vegan dumpling wrappers

Instructions

1. Cut a piece of parchment paper to fit inside of a six or eight-inch bamboo/vegetable steamer. If you use a vegetable steamer; you will need to coat it lightly with some oil.
2. Use the saute setting on the IP. Add the oil/broth and mushrooms; cook for a minute and toss in the carrots, cabbage rice wine vinegar, and soy sauce; saute until the moisture is absorbed.
3. Take the liner out of the IP and set it on the stovetop; mix the sesame oil and ginger.
4. Place the wrapper on a cutting board, spreading water around the edge with your fingertips. Add one tablespoon of the mixture in the middle of the wrapper. Double it in half while matching each of the edges; press together.
5. Place the 12 dumplings on level one of the steamer with the pleated side facing up.

6. Place the top on the steamer (if you are using one); add 1 ½ cups of water to the Instant Pot and lower the contents.
7. Place the lid on tightly making sure the steam release is sealed.
8. Choose the steam function for seven minutes.

Enjoy!

Note: If you are using a bamboo steamer (eight-inch), you can use both layers and make a double batch. Don't worry if the lid won't fit; just leave it off the steamer.

Yields: Provides 12 dumplings (1 per serving)

Biryani Rice

Ingredients

1 minced garlic clove
1 t. cumin seeds
1/4 cup red onion
½ t. turmeric powder
1 cinnamon stick
¼ t. salt
1 cup brown rice
¼ cup raisins
1 ½ cups water
¼ cup tightly packed chopped mint
Garnish: Chopped raw cashews

Instructions

1. Soak the rice a minimum of ten minutes and pour into a fine-mesh strainer to drain thoroughly. Use tap water to rinse. Tap on the strainer to remove all of the excess. Set to the side.
2. Set the Instant Pot to the saute setting to heat for 2 minutes. Add the garlic, onion, cumin seeds, cinnamon stick, and salt to the pot for one minute.

3. Turn the IP off, add the rice, water, and stir.
4. Use the 'multigrain' function for 25 minutes.
5. At that time, quick release—remove the top, add the mint and raisins—stir.
6. Top it all off with some fresh mint leaves and chopped cashews either to the side or on top of your tasty treat!

Lentil and Wild Rice Pilaf

Ingredients

¼ cup each:
- wild/black rice
- brown rice

½ cup green or black lentils

Note: Before time to cook: Soak these ingredients for a minimum of 30 minutes

Vegetable Ingredients

½ C. (finely chopped) medium onion
1 C. mushrooms (sliced)
1 finely chopped celery stalk
3 garlic cloves (pressed, minced)

Spice Ingredients

1 t. each:
- Dried coriander
- Fennel seeds

1 Tbsp. Italian blend (no-salt added)
¼ t. red pepper flakes
1 bay leaf
½ t. ground black pepper
2 C. vegetable broth

Instructions

1. Mix the rice and lentils in a medium container; then soak covered with water, thirty minutes ahead of time.
2. Using the high heat setting, sauté the vegetables for three to five minutes; adding water if needed to prevent sticking.
3. At the end of the time, drain and add the spices, and vegetable broth.
4. Lock down the lid for 9 minutes using the high-pressure setting. Do the natural release.
5. Stir the pilaf and let it sit until it absorbs more of the liquid.
6. Serve with some steamed or fresh vegetables.

Yields: Four to Six Servings

Mango Dal

Ingredients

1 C. chana dal (see note)
1 Tbsp. coconut oil
1 medium minced onion
1/2 t. cumin seeds
1 t. sea salt
1 t. ground coriander
4 minced garlic cloves
1/8 t. cayenne pepper
1 Tbsp. minced fresh ginger
4 C. Vegetable broth
2 mangos (peeled and diced)
1 t. ground turmeric or 1 Tbsp. freshly grated turmeric
½ C. fresh chopped cilantro
Juice of ½ of a lime

Instructions

1. Use a colander to thoroughly rinse the dal until the water is running clear.

2. Use the sauté function to heat the coconut oil. After it melts, add the cumin and continue sautéing about thirty seconds or until it begins to get brown. Blend in the ginger, coriander, garlic, sea salt, and cayenne; sautéing for another minute.
3. Add the vegetable broth, dal, and turmeric to the Instant Pot. Continue sautéing until the mixture boils while removing any foam that collects on the top of the mix.
4. Toss in the mangoes, close and lock the lid, and use the beans/chili function for twenty minutes.
5. Let the pressure natural release. Take the top off of the Instant Pot. Pour in the cilantro and lime juice.
6. Serve the tasty meal over a bed of rice.

Note: The chana dal is also known as bengal gram/a lentil which has a nutty and sweet taste. It comes from the kala chana/black chickpeas.

Cooking Tip: You can also prepare the rice at the same time. Put 1 ½ cups of vegetable broth with one cup of basmati rice in a separate dish covered with some aluminum foil or a lid. Set it on top of the dal before closing the lid.

Squash—Peanut Stew

Ingredients

2 Tbsp. peanut oil
1 cup brown rice
2 yellow onions (approximately 2 cups)
1 small green Serrano chili
1 T. fresh grated ginger
1 t. ground cumin
3 garlic cloves
2 t. kosher salt
1-28 ounce can (2 ½ cups) tomato puree
4 C. vegetable broth
1 medium acorn squash

2 T. Each
- chopped roasted peanuts
- brown sugar

½ C. smooth peanut butter

2 Cans black-eyed peas -(16 ounce)

Instructions

1. Finely chop the onions, garlic, and chilies. Rinse the black-eyed peas and drain.
2. Peel, de-seed, and cut the squash into one-inch thick crescents.
3. Using medium heat; pour the oil and onions—sauté approximately fifteen minutes.
4. Mix the garlic, ginger, chili, cumin, and salt. Continue cooking for about five additional minutes. Stir occasionally.
5. Add the tomato puree, broth, acorn squash, peanut butter, and sugar.
6. Continue (on medium) cooking covered for approximately thirty minutes. Add the peas and heat thoroughly.
7. Garnish with the nuts and serve with a dish of rice.

Squash and Rice Casserole

Ingredients

2 tablespoons oil (Not olive because it is a good 'cold' oil)

2 carrots

1 red pepper

2 sticks celery

1 teaspoon fresh/dried thyme

2 crushed garlic cloves

2 to 3 cups vegetable stock

6 to 8 white mushrooms (can omit)

1 (27-ounce) can chopped tomatoes

Small butternut/medium-sized zucchini (Flesh and all of the liquid of squash)

Instructions

1. Peel the squash and chop them into one-inch cubes. Deseed the pepper.
2. Finely chop the onions, carrots, celery, and red pepper. Use a food processor to make the job easier.
3. Use the sauté function to heat the oil on the medium setting. Add the red peppers, celery, onions, and carrots and blend for another minute. Toss in the mushrooms and lastly the rice; mix.
4. In a metal bowl/dish, place the ingredients to fit into the Pot; add 2 to 3 cups of stock (sticky rice) or 1 ¼ cups liquid and one cup of rice, and put it into the IP. Blend in the squash.
5. Pour about 1 ½-inches of water into the Pot and put the dish/bowl on the trivet. Close the lid and place the cooker on the rice setting.
6. Once the time is completed, enjoy your delicious invention.

Note: Olive oil loses its 'value' when it is heated, making it like any other oil.

Steamed Veggies with Capers & Garlic

Ingredients

1 cup water
2 large carrots
Pepper and Sea salt
11 ounces Brussels sprouts

For the Sauce:

1 Tbsp. baby capers
1 Tbsp. fresh chopped parsley
1 ounce unsalted with a pinch of salt or salted butter
2 clove of garlic
1 small lemon peel

2 Tbsp. lemon juice

Instructions

1. Peel and slice the carrots into thick chunks. Cut the Brussels sprouts in half.
2. Add the water to the Instant Pot and put the veggies in an oven-proof container or the steam basket.
3. Use the high-pressure manual setting for two minutes. Perform a natural release for several minutes, and then do the quick release.
4. Meanwhile; add the sauce ingredients except for the lemon juice into a small pot and place over the range using the medium-high setting. Cook for about one minute after the butter has melted—stirring frequently. Take away from the burner and set to the side
5. Use the tongs to take out the basket from the Instant Pot and put the veggies into a serving dish.
6. Drizzle with some of the juice and add the sauce over the top. Yummy!

Yields: Serves Two

White Beans – Mushrooms & Farro

Ingredients

½ cup faro
1 cup dried navy beans
3 cups mushrooms (finely chopped)
2 tablespoons hulled barley
9 garlic cloves (finely chopped)
½ of a jalapeno pepper (chopped)
1 tablespoon each:
- Shallot powder
- Thai red curry paste

2 tablespoons onion powder
Fill the Pot: Water about 1 ½ inches over the ingredients above
2 medium diced tomatoes

Chopped scallions and cilantro

Instructions

1. Choose the 'soup' setting on the Instant Pot, and add all of the ingredients except for the tomatoes, cilantro, and scallions. (Cooks for thirty minutes.)
2. Blend the tomatoes in when the cycle is completed.
3. Garnish with the cilantro and scallions.

Note: If you want more servings, add more mushrooms and another ½ cup of beans

Yields: Three Servings

Whole Wheat Spinach and Pasta

Ingredients

5 cups water
1 pound whole wheat fusilli pasta
4 minced garlic cloves (to taste)
4 cups chopped, frozen spinach
4 tablespoons butter (cubed)
Pepper and salt as desired
½ cup grated Parmesan cheese (see the recipe in Ch. 5 For homemade vegan parmesan)

Garnish: More parmesan cheese

Instructions

1. Empty the water into the Instant Pot along with the pasta and garlic, with the frozen spinach on the top layer.
2. Set the IP using the high, manual function for six minutes. Quick release and open the lid; add the butter, Parmesan cheese, pepper, and salt.
3. Place the top back on the IP, close, and allow the pasta to absorb the juices for about five minutes.
4. Garnish with more Parmesan cheese.

Yields: Eight Servings

Basic Veggies

Mashed Acorn Squash

Ingredients

2 acorn squash (trimmed stem, halved, seeded)
1 tsp. kosher salt
¼ tsp. baking soda
½ C. water
Salt and pepper to taste
2 T. brown sugar
½ t. grated nutmeg
2 T. butter

Instructions

1. Flavor the outside of the squash with some salt and baking soda.
2. Put the cooling rack/steaming basket in the Instant pot with the water, positioning the squash on top.
3. Close the top and begin the high-pressure setting, and cook for twenty minutes.
4. Quick release and remove the acorn squash from the Pot; let it cool. When cooled, remove the skin.
5. Mix in the brown sugar, butter, and nutmeg.
6. Use a potato masher to blend until the squash is smooth.

Yields: Four to Six Servings

Steamed Artichokes

Ingredients

2 medium whole artichokes (About 5.5 ounces)
1 cup of water
1 lemon wedge

Instructions

1. Remove any damaged leaves and wash the artichokes. Cut the stem and top off 1/3 of each artichoke. Use the lemon wedge to coat the artichokes to prevent them from browning too quickly.
2. Place the rack into the Instant Pot and place the artichokes on top. Add the water and close the lid making sure the valve is in the sealed position.
3. Set the manual mode time for twenty minutes. Hit cancel at the end of twenty minutes to turn off the warming function.
4. Wait approximately ten minutes, and open the valve to release the pressure.

Yields: Two to Four Servings

Quick and Easy Baked Potatoes

You can do as many or as few as you wish—up to five pounds.

Instructions

1. Chop or peel the potatoes, so they are all the approximately the same size.
2. Place the steamer rack into the IP. Empty a cup of water into the Pot and toss in the potatoes.
3. Close the lid and be sure it is sealed. Using the manual button; set the time for ten minutes.
4. After about twenty minutes; the pressure will naturally release.

Note: If you prefer a crispy crust, you can also bake them at 350°F for about ten minutes.

Beans

Ingredients

1 Lb. dried beans of your choice (see below)
1 Tbsp. olive oil
8 cups water
2 to 3 garlic cloves
1 to 2 tsp. salt
Optional: 1 bay leaf

Instructions

1. Don't fill the pot more than half full. Add all of the ingredients into the Instant Pot. Secure the top to the sealing position.
2. *Cook the Beans*: You can use the following guidelines to prepare your beans without any preparation other than sorting and washing them.
3. Place the IP on high-pressure for the recommended times as shown below for your choice of beans. Remember, it takes approximately 15 to 20 minutes before the pressure begins to cook.
4. At the end of the time; do the natural release, which is approximately twenty to thirty minutes or do the quick release.

Times for the Beans:

a. Black beans or Black-eyed peas is about 20 to 25 minutes
b. Pinto, Navy or Great Northern Beans are around 25 to 30 minutes
c. Cannellini and Chickpeas (garbanzo beans) should take 35 to 40 minutes

Note: You can let the beans cool in the cooking juices to freeze for up to three months or in the fridge for up to one week.

Baby Carrots

Ingredients

½ tablespoon butter
Pinch of salt
½ cup water
2 cups baby carrots
1 tablespoon brown sugar (Optional)

Instructions

1. Put the brown sugar, butter, salt, and water into the Instant Pot.
2. Use the sauté function and stir until the butter melts (about 30 seconds).
3. Add the carrots and stir. Secure the lid on the cooker, close the valve, and set the steam function for fifteen minutes.
4. After the time is up on the IP; use the quick release function, and take the lid off the Instant Pot. Sauté until the liquid is gone. Take out the carrots and serve.

Glazed Carrots

Ingredients

½ cup water
2 teaspoons butter
1 pound carrots
1 teaspoon honey
1/3 cup brown sugar

Instructions

1. Put the carrots in the bottom of the Instant Pot. Empty ½ cup of water into the Pot.
2. Place the remainder of the ingredients on top of the carrots.
3. Use the manual setting for five minutes.

Delicious!

Corn—Taiwanese Street Food Style

Ingredients

4 (Ears) Corn on the Cob

The Taiwanese Sauce

2 Tbsp. Shacha Sauce
1 Tbsp. sugar or substitute
3 Tbsp. Light soy sauce
¼ t. sesame oil
1 t. garlic powder

Instructions

1. Preheat the oven to 450°F.
2. Empty one cup of cold tap water into the Pot.
3. Place the basket/trivet in the bottom and put the corn on it.
4. Set the Pot for one to two minutes on the high-pressure setting.
5. At the end of the cycle; turn off the Instant Pot and quick release, opening the lid slowly.
6. Combine the sauce ingredients in a small mixing container.
7. Brush the sauce over the corn with a basting brush.
8. On a baking tray, place the corn and put it on the oven rack for about five to ten minutes.

Yields: Serves Two to Four

Instant Pot Cranberry Sauce

This is one of those recipes that can be used for holidays, as a spread, a dessert topping.

Ingredients

2 ½ teaspoons orange zest
¼ cup orange juice
12-ounces cranberries (divided)

Optional: Pinch of salt

2 Tbsp. Honey or maple syrup
½ to 1 cup sugar (vegetarians use a ½ cup of a substitute such as Stevia)

Instructions

1. Prepare the cranberries by removing the stems and rinsing them under running cold water. Throw away any of the shriveled or discolored berries.
2. Combine the orange juice and maple syrup in the Instant Pot.
3. Toss in approximately 10-ounces of the cranberries and orange zest.
4. Close the lid and cook for one minute (+) seven using the natural release.
5. Use caution when you open the top and do not get burned by the steam.
6. *For the Sauce*: Turn the IP to medium heat and blend in the berries with ½ cup of the white sugar (Vegetarians use ¼ cup Stevia/another substitute). Use some salt and a bit more sugar for additional flavor.
7. *Adjust to your taste and enjoy!*

IP Green Beans

Ingredients

½ tablespoon butter
 A pinch of pepper and salt
1 pound green beans

Instructions

1. Put the rack in the Instant Pot. Empty a cup of water in the IP.
2. Place the beans in the pot and cook for three minutes.

Serve with the butter or other preferred toppings.

Note: If you like softer green beans, you should continue cooking them for an additional five minutes (or so).

Kale and Carrots

Ingredients

1 tablespoon of fat or ghee
10-ounces of kale
1 thinly sliced medium onion
5 garlic cloves (peeled and sliced thin)
3 medium carrots (½-inch slices)
Kosher salt
Aged balsamic vinegar
½ cup chicken broth
Black pepper
¼ teaspoon red pepper flakes: *Optional*

Directions

1. Slice away the ribs from the kale and roughly chop them.
2. Using the medium heat setting, add the ghee into the pot. Blend in the onions and carrots and sauté until softened. Toss the mixture and continue to sauté for about 30 seconds.
3. Pour the broth in and add the pepper, salt, and kale.
4. Set the Instant Pot heat to high, close the top, and set the timer for eight minutes.
5. At the end of the time, let the pressure drop naturally which should be between ten and fifteen minutes.
6. Take the lid off, and stir;

7. taste to see if you need more seasonings.

You can add some red pepper flakes give it a splash of balsamic vinegar.

Note: Be sure there is a minimum of at least one-third 'head-space' in the top of the cooker - or it could explode.

Yields: Serves Two

Instant Pot Mushrooms

Ingredients

16 ounces (or so) button or cremini mushrooms
6 finely chopped clove of garlic
½ of 1 red onion (chopped)
¼ cup low-sodium soy sauce
½ cup mushroom or vegetable stock

Directions

1. Place all of the components on the list into the Instant Pot. Securely close the lid, setting it manually for four minutes. Do a quick release.
2. If the sauce needs to be thickened; use the sauté function. Let the juices come to a boil. Combine two to three tablespoons of cornstarch with ¼ cup of water, mix and add the slurry. Continue stirring and sauté for one minute.
3. Enjoy as a garnish to some potatoes or rice.

Curried Spring Vegetable Potato Chaat

Ingredients

4 medium russet potatoes
¼ tsp. salt
2 tsp. to 1 tablespoon olive oil
¼ to ½ tsp. Indian curry powder (garam masala)

Vegetable Curry Ingredients

1 ½ tsp. garam masala/another Indian curry blend
1 Tbsp. olive oil/other mild oil
½ tsp. ground turmeric
½ tsp. cumin seeds or ¼ teaspoon ground cumin
¼ tsp. ground mustard powder
1 tsp. minced garlic
1 Tbsp. grated ginger
¼ tsp. ground cinnamon
1 cup each:
- carrots
- zucchini
- bell pepper

½ cup water (maybe more if needed)
Reserved potato from the cooked potatoes
Salt to taste
2 cups of greens (Ex. Collards, spinach, kale or rainbow chard)

The Cucumber Cilantro Raita Ingredients

2 Tbsp. Minced cilantro
2 Tbsp. Grated cucumber
¼ cup plain yogurt/unsweetened plain soy yogurt
Pinch of salt

Garnishes

Chopped scallions, cilantro, or cashews

Instructions

1. Peel and slice the potatoes in half lengthwise. Slice the carrots. Chop the bell peppers.
2. Prepare two baking sheets with parchment paper. Heat the oven to 425°F.
3. Rub the potatoes with some olive oil placing them cut-side down. Sprinkle the tops with the salt and garam masala.

4. Put into the oven for 30 to 45 minutes. Let them cool until you can easily handle them. Scoop out the insides, leaving some of the outsides to serve as a bowl with a 'bowl lip.'

5. *In the Instant Pot*, set the sauté function—adding the oil to heat up. Add the cumin seeds, garam masala, turmeric, cinnamon, and mustard powder. Continue sautéing for one minute.
6. Pour in the water and carrots, closing the lid and pressure valve. Use the high-pressure setting for five minutes.
7. Release the pressure by moving the valve to vent; use caution with the steam. Remove the top and add the potato and zucchini.
8. Switch the function back to sauté. Add a little more water if needed. Once they are tender; add the chard and continue sautéing for one minute.
9. *Make the Raita* by stirring in the cucumber, yogurt, and cilantro—adding salt if desired.
10. Fill the potato bowls/skins with the curry mixture and enjoy with your choice of toppings.

Yields: Eight Servings

IP Potato Salad

Ingredients

2 to 2 ½ Lbs. potatoes
4 large eggs
1 ½ cups of water

For the Dressing:

2 tablespoons fresh parsley
1 Tbsp. Yellow mustard
¾ cup light olive oil mayonnaise (see Ch. 5 for Mayonnaise recipe—vegetarian)
1 minced dill pickle spear
¼ cup scallions (the white sections) or onions

1 chopped rib of celery
1 tsp. each:

- seasoned salt
- sea salt

The Garnish: ½ to 1 tsp. paprika
Optional: 1 Tbsp. fresh dill weed

Notes: Try this for a change of pace:

Instructions

1. Before time to cook, prepare the raw potatoes using a 30-minute soak.
2. Put the eggs and potatoes into the steamer/trivet basket with the 1 1/2 cups of water.
3. Close the pressure valve and lock the top. Cook four minutes using high-pressure.
4. In the meantime, blend the dressing ingredients, and set them to the side for now.
5. After the beep; do a quick release.
6. Place the eggs in a pan of cool/ice water—then peel. Mince or dice the eggs and combine with the potatoes.
7. Pour the dressing mixture and mix thoroughly.
8. Cover the dish—chill before serving.

Indian Potato Salad

Ingredients

2 cups water
2 Pounds red potatoes (bite-size pieces)
1 cup each:

- Carrots
- Green peas (fresh/thawed frozen)

Saute Ingredients

1 t. coriander seeds
2 Tbsp. Olive oil (Your choice of another mild oil)

½ t. mustard seeds
1 t. minced garlic
1 ½ t. each:
- garam masala
- cumin seeds

Mint Chutney – Cilantro Ingredients

½ cup each:
- Fresh cilantro
- Mint leaves

½ knob fresh ginger (cut into pieces)
2 teaspoons lime juice
¼ cup water
½ teaspoon salt
Optional: 1 ½ cups cooked chickpeas

Instructions

1. Pour the water, carrots, and potatoes into the Instant Pot.
2. Set on high-pressure for ten minutes. Manually release the pressure at the end of the time and take the lid off of the Pot.
3. Toss the peas in the Pot and set the low pressure for zero (yes 'o') and lock the lid.
4. Once the pot is back to pressure, release manually and place everything in a colander. Thoroughly rinse them using cold water. Set to the side
5. Over medium heat, using a sauté pan; pour the oil, coriander, cumin, and mustard seeds sautéing for about two minutes.
6. Reduce the heat and toss in the garlic and garam masala. Saute for one more minute and remove from the burner. Cool.
7. Add the mint chutney – cilantro ingredients to a processor, pulsing until smooth.
8. Using an over-sized container; add all of the components, mixing well.
9. You can chill for an hour or eat it now.

Yields: Four to Six Servings

IP Perfect Rice

Ingredients

1 cup each water and Jasmine Rice

Instructions

1. Gently scrub the rice with some cold water and discard the water; continue rinsing until the water stays clear.
2. Pour in the water and rice to the Instant Pot. Close the top and cook three minutes using high pressure.
3. Use the natural release for ten minutes; release the remaining pressure and open the lid.

This is perfect rice every time!

Mexican Green Rice

Ingredients

1 ¼ C. low-sodium vegetable broth
1 C. uncooked long-grain rice
Flesh of ½ avocado
¼ cup green hot sauce or green salsa
½ cup fresh cilantro

Instructions

1. Empty the rice and broth into the Instant Pot, stir, and lock it down choosing the high-pressure cycle for 3 minutes.
2. After the beep, turn the cooker off and allow the ten-minute natural pressure release. After that, do a quick release. Fluff it with a fork.
3. In a blender, combine the salsa, cilantro, and avocado with a little water making it with a sour cream consistency.

4. Stir the rice into the mixture and add some pepper and salt for additional flavoring.

Yields: Three Cups

Instant Pot Spaghetti Squash

Ingredients

1 cup water
1 spaghetti squash

Instructions

1. Cut the squash lengthwise and remove the seeds.
2. Pour one cup of water in the Instant Pot.
3. Begin by stacking the squash on top of each other with the cut side of the squash upwards. Close the top with the vent closed. Use the manual function for five minutes on the high-pressure setting.
4. When the time is complete; release the steam waiting for about five minutes until most of the steam dispels. Open the lid and test the squash for doneness.

Sweet Potatoes

Ingredients

1 cup cold tap water
2 Lbs. of sweet potatoes
¼ teaspoon nutmeg
2 tablespoons maple syrup
2-3 tablespoons unsalted butter
Fine Sea Salt

Instructions

1. Peel and cut the potatoes into one-inch chunks.
2. Empty the water into the Instant Pot and place the basket in the bottom of the unit.

3. Cook using the high-pressure function for eight minutes.
4. Turn off the heat; do a quick release and open the top.
5. Put the potatoes in a big container. Using a potato masher; squash the potatoes. Toss in the unsalted butter, nutmeg, and syrup.
6. Mash the potatoes to the desired creaminess and season with a pinch of salt.

Yields: Two to Four Servings

Chapter 5: Sauces, Salsa & More

There is not any reason to worry about what is in your condiments. These are some homemade substitutes you can use with your unique meal planning with your Instant Pot.

Marinara Sauce

Ingredients

½ cup red lentils
1 cup large sweet potatoes (diced) (about 2)
2 (28-ounce) cans crushed tomatoes with basil
1 teaspoon salt
1 ½ cups water
2 to 3 minced garlic cloves

Instructions

1. Prepare the lentils; removing any ones that are shriveled, and rinsing them in a fine mesh strainer.
2. Use the sauté function with medium heat on the Instant Pot; add the salt, garlic, lentils, and sweet potatoes for two minutes.
3. Pour the water and tomatoes into the Pot, mixing well.
4. Use the high-pressure setting for 13 minutes. Perform the natural release; remove the lid.
5. Stir and puree with an immersion blender if you have one.

Yields: Two Quarts

Vegan Mayonnaise

Ingredients

1 t. fresh lemon juice
½ C. soy milk
1 C. canola, safflower, or olive oil
Pinch of ground mustard and salt

Instructions

1. Blend the soy and the juice with a wand blender or regular blender for 30 seconds.
2. Slowly pour in the oil until it thickens.
3. Add the mustard and salt, and blend.

Vegan Mozzarella Balls—Buffalo Style

Ingredients

2 tablespoons agar powder
1 cup water
1 teaspoon pectin
2 tablespoons tapioca starch
1 ½ cups plain soy yogurt
¼ teaspoon guar gum/substitute with xanthan gum
1/4 cup raw organic melted coconut oil
Pinch of sea salt
Ice-cold water in a large container

Instructions

1. Use a large pot—add the water and agar powder—bringing it to a boil. Continue stirring the ingredients until the agar is liquefied and take the pot off of the burner.
2. Blend in the tapioca. Transfer the mix to a food processor/blender. Pour in the soy yogurt, guar gum, salt, and pectin. Blend until creamy smooth.

3. With the unit running—toss in a small amount of coconut oil—continue blending again until blended.
4. Use a small cookie scoop to make the mozzarella balls. Drop them into the ice water container. Let them set for two or three minutes.
5. Store them in containers where they are not crowded one on top of the other.

Use this on any dish you desire.

Yields: Serves Six

Vegan Parmesan Cheese

Ingredients

Zest of 1 small lemon
¼ cup nutritional yeast flakes
1 cup raw pine nuts/raw cashews
1 tsp. garlic powder
½ tsp. dried Italian herbs
½ tsp. sea salt (little slight)

Instructions

1. Use some parchment paper to line a cookie sheet.
2. Preheat the (regular) oven to 300°F.
3. Pulse the pine nuts/cashews to a fine texture; be careful to not over-process. Add everything together.
4. Empty the mixture onto the prepared cookie sheet and bake for 25 minutes—stirring from time to time. Take it out of the oven and let it cool.

Sprinkle on your favorite Instant Pot recipe.

Note: The "cheese" keeps in the refrigerator in a closed jar for up to one month.

Yields: 1 ¼ Cups

Raw Food Salsa

Ingredients

Juice of half a lime
2 cups small chopped tomatoes
1-2 pressed minced clove of garlic
¼ tsp. sea salt

Optional Ingredients:

1 tsp. chili pepper or jalapeno pepper
¼ tsp. cayenne pepper
1 Tbsp. minced red onion
½ tsp. each:
- Chili powder
- Ground cumin

2 Tbsp. minced fresh cilantro

Instructions

1. Combine the minced garlic, chopped tomatoes, lime, and sea salt.
2. Add any of the optional ingredients you want.
3. Blend well and chill until ready to serve.

Yields: Eight Servings or Two Cups

Chapter 6: Snacks and Desserts

IP Applesauce

Ingredients

1 cup water
6 to 8 medium to large apples
1 to 2 drops cinnamon essential oil or
1 teaspoon cinnamon

Instructions

1. Wash the apples and take out the cores of each one. Cut into two-inch chunks. Put in the Instant Pot with one cup of water.
2. Close the lid, and set the timer for eight minutes on the high-pressure setting with the steam vent sealed.
3. The pot will take approximately eight minutes to reach its ultimate high- pressure, and will cook the eight minutes. Let the applesauce set for two to three minutes after the buzzer goes off. Release the pressure and open the top. Remove an excess of water.
4. Use an immersion blender or electric mixer to get the sauce to the desired consistency. Add one to two drops of the cinnamon powder or cinnamon oil.
5. Let it cool and refrigerate.

Note: The Gala, Granny Smith, and Fuji apples work best for this recipe. Make any alterations to suit your specific needs; it is delicious!

Cranberry and Pears Cake

Dry Ingredients

1 ¼ cups whole wheat pastry flour
½ teaspoon each:
- Ground cardamom
- Salt
- Baking powder
- Baking soda

Wet Ingredients

½ cup unsweetened non-dairy milk
¼ cup whole earth sweetener agave 50
2 tablespoons each:
- Ground flax seeds
- Olive oil

Mix-Ins

½ cup fresh chopped cranberries
1 cup diced pears

For Cooking

1 ½ cups water

Instructions

1. Lightly grease a six or seven-inch bundt pan and set it to the side.
2. Add the insert and water into the bottom of the Instant Pot.
3. Using a medium mixing container, blend all of the dry ingredients. In an over-sized measuring cup, add the entire list of the wet ingredients. Blend in all of the mix-ins.
4. Spread the batter into the prepared pan and cover with a layer of aluminum foil.

5. Place in the Pot with the steam rack. Close the top with the vent closed. Use the high-pressure setting for 35 minutes.
6. At the end of the time; do a natural release. Take the lid off and lift the cake out of the Pot, taking off the foil.
7. Let the cake cool before attempting to remove it from the pan.

Yields: Four to Six Servings

Conclusion

Thank you again for downloading your personal copy of the Instant Pot Cookbook For Vegetarian Legends ®: Pressure Cooker Guide!

I hope the Instant Pot Cookbook For Vegetarian Legends ®: Pressure Cooker Guide was able to help you to with all of the tools you need to achieve your goals throughout your new experiences with your new cooker.

The next step is to choose and test some of these delicious recipes and surprise your family and friends. You can now prepare healthy, quick, and easy recipes without all of the worries with the time-consuming task of meal preparation.

You will soon discover why so many people continue to use this fantastic kitchen aid. After all, it covers all of these areas

- *Energy Efficiency*
- *Dependable and Safe*
- *Convenience*

Lastly, if you learned some new information and gained insight on how much healthier your lifestyle can become as a vegetarian; then I'd like to ask you for a tremendous indulgence.

Would you kindly leave a personalized assessment of how much you believe this book has helped you with your new lifestyle on Amazon? It is so valued!

Thank you and good luck!

Made in the USA
Middletown, DE
20 November 2017